Table of Contents

FOREWORD

As a businessman and entrepreneur I'm continually amazed that the public in general, politicians and a lot of business colleagues seem unable to grasp that life, business and markets are a constantly evolving process.

We often hear that we should save the "this" or prop up the "that". We are told that we don't make anything anymore or that losing an industry type is a blow to the economy. Most people, though, never stop and say "but why is business changing? What is influencing markets? How does this affect me going forward?" Despite all the industry losses, the collapsing of certain market segments in 2016, we now have more people in employment at 31 million, more businesses than ever at 5.5 million and higher wages and better lifestyles. This is evolution in action.

The impact of technology always has been a driving factor in change. David's book is an important road map for those of us in business that want to still be here, trading and growing and making a difference in the years to come.

Paul Andrews - CEO Jobs in Kent and Host of the Business Bunker Radio Show

INTRODUCTION

The title of this book may be a little forward, or even aggressive, but this is honestly how I feel about just how much the business landscape has changed and continues to change further.

I do understand just how scary this must be for business owners; to date businesses have been built from a very solid set of rules and understanding. However, the new business landscape does not recognize these rules and is re-writing them daily.

It used to take years for a brand to be built, many hours of hard graft and paying your dues to become a respected and trusted business. Today, brands and businesses are being built in months, if not weeks. Getting your message across and out there to large amounts of people used to take years; yet today a single piece of content can be seen by tens of thousands of people in just a few hours. The speed that a business can be built does not excuse the graft, quality and trust that still must exist in all businesses.

It will be no surprise for you to hear that technology is at the very heart of all this disruption. Keeping up to date and ahead of the curve is no mean feat. But keeping an eye on tomorrow and taking action is what is going to keep you in business for the next five to ten years.

This is not a book about social media, although I will cover that, nor is it a book about cloud computing, again covered. This is a book about what has changed and what you, the small business owner, needs to know in order to position your company ready to meet the needs of the modern worker and the modern consumer.

There will be no jargon or technical information being shared, this is your handbook to make the changes required or at least understand them and see how they could be applied to, and benefit, your company.

Change can be seen as scary but this is deep in our DNA as a species. Humans were never the strongest or the fastest on this planet. What we do have is the ability to adapt to our environment over millions of years. It's time to evolve.

I will be building a companion course to go with this book and as a thank you purchasing I would like to invite you to get free access to this. To do so visit www.davidmarkshaw.com/book-course

ABOUT THE AUTHOR

David Shaw is an author, public speaker and technology savvy entrepreneur. Being born in April 1979 has enabled him to witness, firsthand, the rise of technology and how it has impacted business. David worked in both blue chip and small technology companies in his early career and also had roles in sales and marketing in the late nineties and early 2000s. More recently David has worked with technology start-ups and marketing companies and is currently head of digital for a large group of companies based in Kent. David is a keen blogger and podcaster and continues to produce educational content on the subject of merging sales and marketing teams through digital and how technology impacts small business owners. You will often find David as a speaker on many digital marketing event line-ups, including Social Day and New Media Europe to name a few. You can find out more about David and his work at www.davidmarkshaw.com

CHAPTER 1 - THE START

This book is the combination of the last 10 years of my professional career. I have been fortunate enough to work in some amazing companies across a variety of sectors. The combination of this has given me an insight into where the future of business is and what we need to do to be ready. I always like to take a trip back and understand where we have come from in order to give context to where we are heading. So, with that in mind, let's take a quick look at the last 15- 20 years of the small business landscape.

Until five years ago, there were not many changes and what changes there were came about gradually. For example, the introduction of the personal computer was a big change. At first it was a single computer in an office and only skilled operators were supposed to use it. Then as the PC became more cost effective, and easy to use, it slowly became the main stay of every desk in every business.

The other was the fixed line telephone and fax that would soon become standard in every office. At this time work was completed in the office as that was really the only place it could be done - with the exception of sales people; these people had the pleasure of driving to client's offices and giving presentations. There was a need for this because the sales person had the knowledge; they had all the information about their product or service.

Companies would promote themselves via advertising and trade shows and this is how we got to learn about other companies and new products and services.

There was also direct mail and outdoor advertising and, if you had the budget, you could even use radio and TV advertising to reach large audiences. The audiences were there because TV was scheduled and our attention was still quite high at this point in time.

The most popular marketing tactic was telemarketing, and at the time it worked. You called up companies promoting your products and services hoping to find someone who was either looking to buy or could be interested. Business was quite simple; if you kept your message frequency high and relevant it would keep you top of mind for prospects and enable you to keep winning new business. It was, of course, more complex than that sentence but that was the overall objective.

For interested prospects they would either speak to the company via phone or in person if at a trade show. In some cases, for more complex sales, there would be a meeting or a demonstration. This was the era of people-to-people sales and the "always be closing" sales person. The people-to-people element is still, and always will be, a huge factor. It is how we connect with each other that has changed.

If you go back a little further into the late 1950s and 1960s, people were educated by products via heavy advertising. Some of it quite suspect as to where the truth was, but people believed it. There were so few channels, TV, radio, print and outdoor that getting your message out there was a good way of raising awareness and getting sales.

Email became mainstream in the early 1990s and added a welcome layer to the communication setup. As the Internet was becoming more and more prevalent we could start to see the first signs of change. Email gave us an instant response and an exciting new way to communicate. Although feared by many at the start, it was the same fear of the fax machine: that someone might intercept it. We soon got over this fear and were soon sending hundreds and thousands of emails every day. At first, every single email was not just opened but read completely. Getting an email was exciting, almost like getting a personal letter.

This was just the very start and we had little idea what was about to happen at a furious and fast rate. Sure we had websites but they were static and only contained basic information - almost like an online brochure. They often had animated gifs (the moving icons) and were set up and forgotten about. Nobody was going to look at it. Why would they when they could email us or speak to us? There was not much content on the internet originally and it was considered something for the techies and the geeks, certainly not for the mainstream.

As for people and jobs, we have come from an era where most people were taught that if you worked hard at school and college (and in some but not all cases you went to university and got a degree) then you were set for life. For many people they would get a job and stay at that company until they retired. Even for those that did change jobs on occasion, it was few and far between with maybe three to five changes throughout their career. We were sold a promise and a dream and this was the case for decades.

Over the next few years there were some more subtle but telling changes. We had more computers and now servers in-house. Software was expensive to own and install, as was the cost of training and support. Only those companies with money could afford the best software. Smaller companies made do with spreadsheets.

Mobile phones were introduced in 1985 but had a very slow uptake and only 7% of the market owned a mobile phone over the first 10 years. It was 1999 when the tipping point was reached and then it rose sharply to 46%. This was also the year that the term web 2.0 was coined which basically meant we would soon start creating websites that were interactive and not just static. From 1999 onwards we have seen some dramatic changes in both technology and business and also the way we communicate and buy and sell anything. It is fair to say the last 15 -16 years have seen more change than at least the 50 years prior, if not more.

As for you, the small business owner the last 5 years or so have been pretty transformational and everything we knew about business is being challenged. Business is changing, communication is changing and people are changing. I understand how difficult it must be to try to manage and adapt to so much change in such a short space of time. Technology was something that was outsourced or a role for someone for slightly larger companies. IT was supposed to be an enabler and not something that drives your business. Now the conversation around technology and all it touches is prevalent in every boardroom around the country. Regardless of what industry you are in, technology either plays a part or is disrupting what you do. Understanding how technology impacts your business and your industry is the key to a successful future.

CHAPTER 2 - ATTENTION

There is one major change that the recent technology advances has resulted in and that is attention. In 2012, the average human attention span was around 12 seconds, compared to that of the humble goldfish which is said to be 8 seconds. In 2015 a human's attention span was around 7 seconds long. The reason? In a few words - mobile phones. It is not that we have less attention than we did; we just have far more fighting and competing for our attention. Therefore, if something does not grab and hold our attention very quickly, we get distracted and become aware that there are other things we could be doing or checking.

Every spare few seconds we have now, we check our mobile. For email, social media updates, sports scores, games and app notifications. In fact it's notifications from various apps and in-boxes that keep us hooked on checking them every 6 minutes. We spend, on average, three and a half hours a day on our mobile devices, that's 1 day a week. We check them for notifications around 1500 times a week. Sound high? Think about it for a minute; now take a mental note every time you do check it and you will see just how hooked on our mobile devices we now are.

This is driven by what is known as FOMO or fear of missing out. Our brains are now trained to seek new information as soon as our attention is broken. We have multiple social media accounts and multiple email accounts, plus text messages and voice-mails and let's not forget the good old fashioned phone call.

It is already the case that a phone call is annoying - we would rather be sent a text and therefore be able to respond in our own time, than be interrupted and have to talk when someone else dictates. This is going to become more prevalent as we value time more and more. You may recognize yourself in these statements? It is quite a scary thought just how insular we are becoming as we live out more and more of our lives in the digital channels and less in the real world. This book is not about debating if this is right or wrong, but for you to recognize that it is so. Not only is this now the norm but it is not going back ... ever.

There are so many things fighting for our attention today. We receive tons of notifications, emails and messages across a number of devices. We are also trying to keep up to date with what is going on with friends and family on social networks.

What happened before social networks? We only really got updates in person or via email. But now everyone has multiple publishing platforms they can post anything they want to. This has led to even more information to process, react and respond to. People today find themselves checking Facebook as the last thing they do at night and the first thing they do in the morning. It has become a habit. Next time you are in a meeting, or out to dinner with a group of friends, watch what everybody does at the end of the meeting or at a natural pause when out to dinner? Everybody will check their mobile phone without question.

In regards to how this affects business, it is really quite clear. Understanding that your prospects have less time and even less attention than ever before. As we value time more and more and seek to achieve more with less, we will change the way we previously did things in order to give us more time to do what we want and when we want.

We now have hundreds of TV channels and less attention, so how well does TV advertising work today? Even when watching TV do you have a second screen somewhere within an arm's length? And what is the first thing you are doing when the adverts come on? That's right, you pick up your mobile phone. Checking in, seeing what's happened and what you might have missed. These check in moments are very regular and happen at every given opportunity. More often than not, we are picking up the remote and fast forwarding through TV adverts as well; with more and more TV being watched on demand. We now expect to be able to watch what we want when we want, from wherever suits us and on any device. The rules have changed completely. Being able to consume what we want when we want is now possible. We live in an on demand, always on, 24/7 world. This has led to less scheduled programming being consumed and far more "binge" watching. No longer do you have to wait for the next episode, next week. You simply wait a second for Netflix to stream the next episode there and then.

Other media is also suffering, such as traditional print. We can get access to pretty much any media we want online and on whatever device we want, so picking up print magazines is even less likely. Newspapers' information is now old as it happened yesterday in most cases. As for adverts in print, do people really look for suppliers in print or do they search online? Our attention has never been under more attack from so many people and companies trying to get in front of us. This has not stopped small businesses still advertising in print. Often packages are sold for both print and online to give you even more reach. There are of course some generations that may still consume print and if that is your target market then print is still a good option and will still get some results. That said, my Nan is in her eighties and is quite proficient in paying her bills and completing her shopping online. It is not for everyone but each year more and more people are defaulting to digital channels rather than traditional media types.

Understanding how time and attention poor today's consumers are means that traditional client acquisition models are far less effective. There are places where awareness campaigns using modern advertising can have an effect but you need to ensure your message is timely, relevant and contextual. Trying to push your messages out onto people is becoming less and less effective and yet still many small business owners will plough huge amounts of money into interruption based advertising. This is where you interrupt content people have chosen to consume, with your own advert; you know the types, the pop-up ads with the elusive 'close' button! . This is because people are applying the old methods to new technology. They are going for reach and frequency and see that the internet has options to do this still. Just think about your own Internet browsing habits and then ask if your advert would be a welcome one?

Today's business owners need to create a different type of marketing plan, one that understands the new consumer and meets them where they are, and at a time that makes sense to them.

Once you realize that we are all in the attention game, regardless of what you do or provide, the competitive landscape looks very different. It is no longer as important to worry about the other provider in your town or city. Your challenge now is getting people to pay attention to you in an era where attention is scarce. We fast forward through every single advert on TV that we can. We tap impatiently waiting for the skip advert button on YouTube and most drivers barely look at the road let alone at the roadside adverts. So in a world where nobody is paying attention, how do you gain awareness and new customers?

The truth is there is some attention out there; it's just that there is a limit to how much one person can pay attention to. The question then becomes more about whose attention you want and what they are paying attention to right now?

The era of mass marketing is slowly dying a slow death and now you need to focus your efforts in the niches. Who is your ideal customer and what is the problem that you solve for them? This is more so for business to business efforts than it is business to consumer where you may be trying to reach a much broader audience but still you need to focus on a smaller group in order to get results.

You need to understand where the watering holes and playgrounds that your ideal customers go to for information and inspiration are. What questions do they have and what are the challenges that they are faced with? These watering holes may be online or offline, you need to keep an eye on this as it may change over time.

These are the places where you know your ideal client is spending time and where you need to be present in order to influence and gain attention. This may take some time, as charging into a LinkedIn group and spraying your sales messages is unlikely to go down very well. The old adage of "know, like and trust" still rings as true today as ever, if not more.

You need to think about giving a reason for your prospects and customers to pay attention to you; just publishing content is not going to be enough as most people are now doing this. Why are you different and what is different about your content, products and services? A few years ago it may have been enough to publish content, but today needs more than that; you need to stand out, stand up and make people pay attention. Being vanilla is never going to work. There is so much vanilla out there and we are now filtering that content out in our social streams and avoiding these people in networking events.

Why you, why your product and why now? In order to get the attention your business needs you will now need to position yourself and your business in such a way that your prospect sees value in spending time interacting, engaging and consuming your content, product or service.

You do this by being a utility and a valued part of their story. Understanding the role you play is key to this; more on this in a later chapter.

The takeaway from this chapter is that today's currency is attention. There is more competition for your ideal prospects' attention than anything else and you need to find a way to position your company, people, products or services in such a way that they pay you that attention. This is done by taking the time to understand what they want to achieve or what problem they are looking to solve. What do they get or what happens if you help them do that? Let them know why you care about this problem or challenge. Explain to them how you intend to solve that problem or achieve that goal and let them know that you understand why it is important to them. Listen to your prospects, answer their questions and this will gain their attention.

CHAPTER 3 - THE INTERNET

It will not come as a surprise to hear that the Internet is at the very heart of all of this change. The Internet has changed the way we communicate and connect and, most importantly, the way we consume information. Sure we had books before and we could, if we wanted, go looking for information but it was time consuming and too much work. Today we can get the answer to pretty much any question with a few finger presses on a piece of glass... our smart phone.

The Internet, although no longer particularly new, is really only starting to bring its promise now. Why is this? What we know as the Internet today was first being talked about in 1962. This was just a concept known as the "Galactic Network" by J.C.R. Licklider of MIT. Over the next 20 years there were some major developments in getting data from one place to another and getting computers to talk to each other. It was not until 1992 when Tim Berners Lee invented the World Wide Web (WWW) that things really started to take place. The concept, though, is much older than most people realise

During the late 1990s the first wave of big .com companies started appearing and huge amounts of money were being invested as people were convinced that there was big money to be made. The stock market reacted in the same way and stocks and shares soared. We all know what happened next. It was between 1999 and 2002 the real .com bubble burst and many companies went out of business very quickly. Companies like Geocities that were purchased by Yahoo for over $3 Billion disappeared just a few years later. There were lots more too; Lycos was purchased again in later years for a fraction of the original value. Even companies like Broadcast.com, another Yahoo acquisition for over $5 Billion dollars, now just redirects to Yahoo's homepage. So why did it all go wrong then? There were a number of reasons, things like no real business plan is some cases but the real reason was the lack of understanding and use of the Internet at that time. We used what was known as a dial-up service; the speeds of 14.4k were not uncommon and I remember getting excited about a 56k connection thinking we would never need more. The bottom line was it was not easy for everyone to access the Internet and it was billed by the hour more often than not, meaning the audience was limited. It was the techies that loved it and built on it. Businesses would still use the Internet for email primarily. Now there were some companies, such as EBay and Amazon that survived the dot com bubble and went on to build amazing companies. The real story, however, is in the next wave of companies that arrived.

It was not until the early 2000s that we were first introduced to broadband - high speed Internet. It was also the first time you could use your home phone at the same time as being online, and this was considered game changing. Broadband changed everything and accelerated not just the speed of the Internet but the rate of innovation for new companies. To give you some idea of the speed increase, the lowest advertised Internet speed today is around 8mb which is 8000k; before we were enjoying speeds of just 56k.

This new high speed Internet meant everybody in a small business could use email and companies like YouTube were possible as we now had the speeds to download and watch video over the Internet. Let's also think about what else was happening around the same time. Mobile phones were becoming a must have item for everybody, web 2.0 meant websites were becoming interactive much more than static websites. Google was founded in the very late 1990s and in early 2004 was starting to become a very popular alternative search engine to AltaVista and Yahoo.

Google realized that there was a need to organize the world's online information as we had all very quickly become connected and could connect to websites from all over the world, if we could find it.

This was just the start. We could now access and find unlimited information very quickly and, to the majority, it was affordable. Think about just how significant this is for a minute; before we relied on people, books, newspapers, the TV and radio to give us the information. Now we can access more information that you could possibly understand in just a few clicks.

Of course business was going to change; of course the way we connected and communicated was going to change. The Internet just made it really easy and, more importantly, possible.

The Internet was always about giving people access to the information we wanted, and this is the most important point that most miss. It's not about only giving people the information you want to give them.

Today there are millions of companies that have been created because of how the Internet and access to information has challenged every business model and industry there is. More will continue to be challenged each and every day. This is just the beginning and anywhere there is inefficiency and third parties will be naturally disrupted first.

One of the biggest changes with the Internet was the roll-out of mobile Internet. But before that there was the rise of Wi-Fi which took away the need to be directly connected via a cable. Having the ability to walk around a building with a laptop and remain connected was the very start of something much bigger. Wi-Fi was becoming popular from around the start of the year 2000 and has become a mainstay of every home and office today.

In 1993 the introduction of 2G connectivity on our mobile phones which enabled text messages and WAP Internet access. WAP was really slow and not easy to navigate but was the start. It was the introduction of EDGE or 2.5G that slowly started making a difference but it was 3G that opened the floodgates. 3G was like the difference between 56k modems and broadband; it blew the doors wide open. 3G arrived in the UK in late 2003 but the handsets were not available and it was not until later in 2004 that they became easily available. A few years later, in 2007, the introduction of the first Apple iPhone with its safari browser that displayed the same websites that we got on our desktops, and the start of the app revolution, that things really started to hot up.

The Internet in 2016 is everywhere; we now have at least 3G access in most areas, granted not enough, and in more and more towns and cities we now have 4G coverage which will eventually be rolled out everywhere..

The Internet is now a massive part of our lives, we depend on it personally and professionally. High speed Internet and web 2.0 gave birth to some amazing technology and companies and we will talk more about them in the next chapter.

So where is it all heading next? Well, with access to the Internet just about everywhere it was only a matter of time before it started to get used in other areas; not just computers and mobile phones. We have already started to see the rise of the Internet of things (IOT), where everyday items like our heating systems, TVs and fridge freezers are all connected to the Internet. This is already available today with companies like

NEST (now owned by Google) offering intelligent systems for the home to control temperature, fire alarms and lots more planned for the very near future. The smart home is here and will continue to get smarter and more connected in the next few years. The Internet of things is only just starting and there is so much more to come. It will not be long before you will be in your self-driving car (already invented), using voice commands to turn the oven on and run your bath so everything is perfect before you get in from work.

The Internet means we are connected 24/7 and can answer pretty much any question we want by reaching into our pockets. Our Smart phones are never far from us and are feeding us information all day long. Being connected like this is having a profound effect on us as people and the way we do business. Information is available anywhere, anytime. This is not an age thing either; people of all ages are digital proficient and are realising the amazing power that the Internet can bring.

Without a doubt one of the largest

innovations to come out of the birth of the Internet is, of course, Social Media. We will discuss this and its effect in more detail in later chapters. However it has become integral to our society today and many people are not only reliant but even addicted to it. The idea of not being connected to the Internet can cause some people to get very anxious. Being connected today is like air for some - it's a must have. If you have teenage children you will know this to be true. Have you ever had the internet go down at home with teenagers in the house? It is like the world has ended. This generation have grown up being connected and have learned to communicate via online channels. More and more of these generations are entering the workforce every single day and some are even starting companies and employing people older than you and I. They communicate slightly differently to older generations and could not imagine a world before the internet.

CHAPTER 4 - THE CLOUD

The cloud is one of those terms that has slipped into everyday language very quickly. We even point up when talking about it even though there is no computing going on up there. In fact, in many cases, it's quite the opposite and is below ground. Cloud computing is a result of the Internet. Although a buzz word for the last 7 or 8 years, it's actually not that new.

As soon as the Internet was created we were looking to not just connect but to share information. The cloud is a very simple concept - accessing computing resources from a remote location. The clouds origins are firmly set in the 1960s and we have had various iterations of it over the last 50 years. It is fair to say that cloud computing was a little bit of a late bloomer but that is directly related to the rise and innovation of the Internet. The first sets of corporate computers were a form of cloud computing in the shape of a mainframe. All of the terminals had no processing power; it all resided in the mainframe although in the same building. Each terminal was used as a remote device to access the data and power of the mainframe. We do the same with social media and most Internet based applications. Our device, mobile, tablet or laptop is the terminal and all the power and hard work and heavy lifting is done at the other end.

The first real big name and game changer was Salesforce. In 1999 they launched the first online only CRM (customer relationship management). It was a simple system that was accessed via your browser and meant no software was required. This led the way for software as a service (SAAS) companies and changed the software landscape forever. Shortly after, in 2002, Amazon web services was launched and made cloud computing available to enterprises. Later, in 2006 it launched its elastic compute cloud (EC2) and gave anybody with a credit card access to computing power and resource on demand. There were other technologies involved that also made this affordable and the result was cloud computing was available by the minute, and to anybody.

Why was this so exciting and game changing? Previously only large companies with lots of resources could afford to develop, distribute and support new software due to the high costs of owning, running and maintaining the computers needed. Now anybody can get access to just the resources they need and only pay for when they need it. This changed the rules for everybody. You can increase and decrease computing needs when you need it. Testing didn't mean owning the servers; just turn them on, pay by the minute and then turn them off.

The result - anybody with an idea and a small budget could now develop, sell and distribute software. There are now millions of applications available either on mobile devices as well as over the Internet (SAAS). The model of "pay as you use" has also changed the way we pay for software. Before the rise of cloud computing, software was expensive to own and maintain. It often required installing it on a dedicated server in your office for the main database and then again the software the users use (front-end) on each of the workstations. For many applications a paid annual maintenance contract was essential for updates, in addition to the cost of the consultant required to carry these out. The 90s and early 00s were a great time to be in the software business but not so much for small business owners. Now the tables have turned.

Software used to be 'one size fits all' and if you wanted to make changes it meant cost; this cost was rarely small. There were not many options for your specific industry and if there was it was really expensive. Today, with software development and associated charges at a fraction of the cost, it is all change.

The likelihood is that there are lots of tools and services that are perfect for your industry; there are also thousands of applications that are completely free to use. Some of the free applications are better than the old paid for versions.

What does this mean for small business owners? It means running a small business is easier and cheaper than before. With CRM, project management software, accounting and social media management all available for free or at a very low cost, it is no longer a competitive advantage of the bigger more established brands.

There are also other advantages of cloud based software and computing. No longer is the office the only place you are able to work from.. With any Internet connected device you can access everything that you normally would do from your office PC. The software is not needed on the device nor is the data you are accessing or creating. It's all cloud based and means you can work from anywhere, at any time and on any device.

This used to be something only enterprises could afford but is now available for the small business owner. Today, there are very few reasons to have an on-site server. There is no longer a need for costly contracts with software vendors and there is a vastly more simplified technology infrastructure.

There is, however, a mindset change that

comes with the new technology landscape. Workers are now mobile, business is now mobile. The old ball and chain of the office and the 9-5 is no longer applicable and that comes with some major new ways of thinking about your business.

Cloud computing has disrupted the traditional norm of 'work gets done at work'. Yet hundreds of thousands of small business owners still pay to run an office. Now there are many examples where having an office is essential; there are also new start-ups everyday and even some established companies with hundreds of workers and no office space. Often these virtual companies have employees all over the country and even the world. The Internet enables us to connect and share from anywhere and therefore the traditional boundaries of skills and employment do not really apply. This does, however, take a very different type of leadership and business model that may not suit your business or leadership style.

Having an office or not is one consideration but instead of just ditching the office at least take a look at how much it costs and what it enables you to achieve. Just taking a look at how much space you have and how often it is used is a worthwhile exercise. If you find that 50% of the time desks and meeting room space are empty it may be time to rethink your office.

Line of sight leadership has been present for the last 50 plus years and to change that to an output based leadership is not going to come easily to everybody, and to some it may not come at all. Just because you cannot see people does not mean they are not working and vice versa. Virtual companies that are realising the benefits of remote working and cloud computing are likely to be running leaner and utilizing a much wider talent pool than those that are just operating locally. The question is, are you going to be able to compete with these companies in the future or are you going to *become* one of these companies?

Using project management tools such as Yammer from Microsoft or Podio from Citrix makes collaborating and communicating with remote teams and workers so much easier. I have used these tools and managed remote employees and have found more communication and productivity than when in an office.

Cloud computing has made the world much smaller. It is now a global market place and your competitors are no longer the ones in the same postcode or zip code as you. With services like Amazon and People Per Hour and even Fiverr there are tens of thousands of freelancers ready to complete work for you for as little as $5. There are even more specific market places like 99designs.com where you can use amazingly talented graphic designers from all over the world to pitch and compete for design projects. These are hugely competitive and offer the client a service that would have normally cost thousands of pounds and hours, but now can be managed in one place and for a fraction of the cost. Meaning a local designer now needs to work much harder to remain competitive. .

Cloud computing is still very young and with industries being disrupted every single day with new services and applications that are looking to remove inefficiency and take market share, there is a real rush on right now to find a niche to own and disrupt. Again the question is are you going to wait to be disrupted or be the *disruptor* in your industry? We will cover more on disruption in Chapter 8.

If you would like to read more about cloud computing I have a ebook that will be published on Amazon but as a reader of this book you get for free. To download your free ebook visit www.davidmarkshaw.com/introductiontocl oud or email at david@davidmarkshaw.com

CHAPTER 5 - INFORMATION
AND BIG DATA

Prior to the dawn of the internet, if you wanted to know something you would either look it up in a book or ask someone. You might learn something from TV or radio and even other forms of print but if you did not know how to make the perfect boiled egg you wouldn't make a huge effort to find out other than asking people you knew.

Today that has changed. With our smart phones to hand we can find out the answer to just about anything in a few taps and scrolls.

That information was always available, just not easily accessible. It is no bother to ask Google, Siri or Cortana how to make the perfect boiled egg and looking at videos alone there are 3.7 million results on this exact question.

There are 300 hours of YouTube footage uploaded every minute, nearly 300 billion emails sent each day, 2 million blog posts written and more iPhones are stolen than babies are born every single day.

Scary numbers right? And these ever increasing numbers show no sign of stopping. Information is everywhere and is changing everything.

There is a lot of talk about Big Data and why businesses should care about it. But what exactly is Big Data?

There is no specific volume   that qualifies data   as big; it's actually about the way in which it's structured. Generally big data is lots of unstructured information. What I mean by this is that it is neither organised nor easy to understand or make decisions from.

An example of this could be traffic data; having lots of information about numbers of cars on the roads at any one time is only useful if you have access to more detail, such as which roads are getting the most traffic   and   at   what   times.   Also understanding other factors such as why a normally quiet street is showing heavy traffic use - knowing it was due to a diversion or traffic incident is all information that makes the 'big data' understandable and useful.

In a small business example, understanding your website traffic is an important metric to measure and monitor. But looking at Google analytics unstructured will just give you more questions than answers. However, add a few filters, and some easy on the eye reports and you now have some information that is hopefully both interesting and useful.

We have access to more information than ever before. The ability to ask questions we never could have before is mind blowing.

There is so much data being produced and now being made available to small business owners where does one start? It's not just information from outside of your business which can improve and take your business forward; your own business is producing tons of data and that is the perfect place to start.

Your phone system can probably tell you tons of information you never knew. Your email marketing software will, without a doubt, have very valuable data you were not aware of. Start with the information that is available and easily accessible today and that will take you towards your current goals. If sales are slow, start there; ask why and ask what do we know? Even what do we want to know?

So it is not so much big data you should be concerned about as a small business owner but small data. Manage that first and see what differences you can make to your business from the information you are g already generating.

With so many tools and services today offering us more insight and more data it can be very easy to get overwhelmed or sucked in. Being overwhelmed is to be expected. Being presented with tons of stats and figures may not mean very much at first. To be completely honest the only numbers that really matter are the ones in the bank balance. Leads and sales are the other numbers that we should really care about and if you have them sorted it may be some other metrics.

Again, start with the numbers that matter. For others they may get sucked in. Google analytics can give you mountains of useful information. It is easy to find yourself digging in deeper and deeper. Can this data help you achieve your goals? Yes, in many cases I am sure it can. But if you do not understand the data you are looking at either take a course or hire a consultant to translate it for you. Get a good grip of which data is useful and which data you need to know in order to meet your goals.

Technology is finding new ways of tracking and understanding everything. With marketing automation software you can track every visitor to your website, what they are doing, where they are clicking and how much they are reading. With auto-responders and smart rules set up in your email you can nurture prospects on auto-pilot. Scaling your digital marketing is getting smarter and easier. This also produces some amazing data and insights.

The sales process is changing as you will see in the next chapter.

What all of this data gives us is a much clearer understanding of the sales process and how well sales and marketing are doing or not doing. Understanding the basics of this is important without a doubt. But what is more important is knowing the right questions to ask. There will be hype and excitement from your marketing team but rather than get over excited about all the new insights, ask the questions that matter. Hundreds of Facebook "Likes" is great, but you cannot pay salaries with them. Thousands of Twitter followers are again brilliant news but the suppliers will not accept them as a form of payment. Don't get me wrong, these are great metrics to have but they are not purchase orders...yet.

As a small business owner you need to ask the difficult questions and have clear goals. Understand how these metrics all lead towards your goals without having to understand the details.

Business is becoming data driven for sure.

But I feel too many people have been blindsided by vanity metrics for the last few years. Large social media followings are great if they are engaged and active with your content and your company. I would rather have 10 twitter followers if those 10 were engaged and interested as opposed to 1000 followers who did not care or see my updates.

Overall, data is something small business owners are going to need to get a grip of if they are to remain competitive. My advice would be to master the small and important data first and then start looking at the other pieces of information your company is, or should be, producing.

What happens if you don't do this? Your competitors are already doing this; maybe not the guys down the street but certainly somebody, somewhere, is trying to take your customers and is using technology and data in a smart way to be more efficient and competitive with either the same product or services as you or with something completely new that renders your products or services obsolete.

Information as a whole has never really had less value as it is everywhere. Understand that once upon a time information was very valuable and now there is a different challenge. Understanding information and making it useful and actionable is where the value lies. What use is collecting all of this information if we cannot understand it nor do anything with it.

This really is the very beginning of the information age and there are very few companies really making maximum use of the data they collect. My advice would be to start small and with the metrics that matter. You do not have to be a data scientist to do this. As a small business owner, you are already dealing with lots of data and it's now just about how you get the most from it.

CHAPTER 6 - THE BUYING PROCESS

This is a subject matter that I am very passionate about. The sales process, for many years, was easy to understand and to operate. I hated it. Disrupt as many people as you possibly could and eventually you would find someone who happened to be looking for exactly what you were selling or were pushed into buying it by overbearing sales people who would not take no for an answer.

"Pound the pavement", "It's a numbers game" and "every no is one step closer to a yes". These were all sayings that were popular amongst sales teams. The one I hate the most though is "always be closing". Close is such a negative word; it implies that there is an end when in fact it is the start. With so much choice now and the ability to tell the world when we get a bad service or when a product is poor, the tables have turned forever. Selling has changed forever. What you need to ask yourself is, "in a world where people can buy from anyone, why should they choose you?"

Traditionally we would find out about new companies, products and services via offline methods. Trade shows, networking, word of mouth, advertising and cold calls. We would then endure the process of trying to extract as much information as we could from the sales person without having to sign anything or agree to a sale. We were reliant on a sales person to give us these answers and we had to trust that what they were saying was, in fact, true.

There were all kinds of tactics used to try to convince the prospect to buy now. It was a real game of cat and mouse. Sales people were considered pushy and their methods pressured. Buyers' remorse was rife and the whole thing was not right. Now there were, and still are, cases of consultative selling where the sales people were decent and honest and did not use these tactics - but unfortunately there were more of the pushy sales people than there were decent ones.

The sales process used to more often than not start with the telesales team. These people would make dozens, if not hundreds, of calls every day in the hope that they would find someone willing to receive some information, agree to a meeting or even buy the product there and then during that call. This practice of cold calling was not for the faint hearted; many times the caller would receive a piece of the recipients mind and exactly what they thought about their methods of selling.

Our time was precious and being interrupted by someone who just wanted to push their product onto us and serve themselves rather than our needs was unwanted, to say the least. This is even truer today.

Trade shows were another way of getting in front of people to demonstrate your amazing product or service. What would happen, though, is people would walk round and try to work out from your banner or leaflets what you did and then translate that into how they could help them achieve their goals. They would have to do this without being collared by the over-eager sales person who prowls the perimeter of their stand waiting to catch the eye of any passerby so they could launch into their sales pitch. What is worse about this is that trade shows are still exactly the same today; nothing has changed except us. We no longer need to go to a trade show to learn about new products or services; we simply reach for our smart phone. In fact, next time you do attend a trade show take a look around. How many people are there just for the keynotes and some networking with people they already know? Then see how many people are on stands looking bored; this is even more noticeable after lunch time when the event generally dies a death. You know it's bad when the exhibitors start going round to other peoples' stands and start pitching to other exhibitors.

You can find out about new products, services and companies from your smart phone and that is, more often than not where the sales process starts today - on a mobile phone and with a search. In most cases it's not a direct search for a product but, in fact, a question. If we have a question we simply ask it to our search engine of choice. Google have called this "The Zero

Moment of Truth".

The Zero Moment of Truth or ZMOT is a really important change in our buying habits and behaviour. We know that, in a heartbeat, we can find out the answer to pretty much any question we want. This has changed the way we buy forever and here is why. Where previously the sales process included a lot of the research and education to take place in person with the sales person, the sales person would need to win the trust of the prospect while moving them towards a sale. Now the prospect is able to educate themselves in their own time and ask as many questions as they want and need without feeling pressured and being sold to.

In fact, ZMOT has evolved even further since that report was published and they are now talking about micro moments of truth.

These are the tiny transactions you make with Google every day and ask the following types of questions:

I want to know…
I want to go……

I want to buy…..
I want to do……

We are now trained to look for these answers all day every day on our smart phones or whatever device is in front of us at the time.

This leaves the ultimate question "if you are not answering those questions, who is?" Most likely a competitor in some shape or form. Are you answering those questions and every single one of them? Are they engaging with your content and your brand?

The sales process today is very different; prospects are discovering and learning about new brands, products, services and people - all in their own time on whatever device they have in front of them and they have the ability to find out what everyone else thinks about it too.

As much as 70% of the buying process will take place online before a sales person is engaged with. The next question is how do you ensure it is your sales person they engage with, or at least your company?

It is still trust at the root of this, as well as all the other factors such as product, place and price. So how do you win that trust? . You need to be answering the questions your prospects have and in the places they expect and want it.

The new sales process also means the ultimate case studies are out there - your customers. The Zero Moment of Truth is that moment your customer is so happy with your product or service, and ultimately the experience, that they tell others.

This could be on social media; it could be on review sites; it could be telling their friends, family and business connections in person.

This is the content that your new prospects are going to find and hear about. This is also true if their experience is a poor one.

The sales process is no longer finished with the prospect signing a contract or handing over the credit card. It now needs to extend to ensuring the customer is delighted and felt looked after and supported. This is what is going to win you new customers or lose you both..

No longer can companies provide a poor service and get away with it. The internet is full of horror stories of how poorly people were treated and this information can be found with a simple search and a few clicks.

Think about your own buying experience when choosing a hotel to stay at. Would you not check them out on TripAdvisor first? Now to be fair, TripAdvisor needs to be navigated with a little caution - as do all review sites. But there is enough information for you to decide for yourself if this is the hotel for you.

Often, negative reviews can lead to more sales if the context is understood. Boutique hotels are not always child friendly and this is often why many stay there. Seeing negative reviews from families only re-enforces the reasons you might want to stay there.

The other thing that is missed in most marketing strategies today is the role we play in the sales process. We are not the hero in the story any longer. For years, companies would tell the world how wonderful they were and why you should buy from them. They were positioning themselves as the hero in the story. Their product or service would save the day is what they promised.

Today a very different story needs to be told. Your prospect or your customer is the hero and not in your story but theirs. Our job is to understand that story and the role we play. What is the objective, pain, problem or goal your prospect is looking to solve or meet? What does it mean to your prospect to meet or solve that and what happens after? Then finally if and how can your product or service help them achieve this and make them the hero in their own story?

It may sound odd but we are telling ourselves many stories every single day. We don't think about our supplier's narrative do we? We are thinking about ours. It might be hard to hear but in most cases our customers do not care about us and our goals although that could change depending on the relationship, circumstances and how a new story of theirs might just work with ours.

Buying is becoming easier too; a few clicks on your phone and you can have things gift wrapped and sent to your home or your shopping delivered or ready to collect. This ease of buying is the reduction of friction in the sales process.

Are you making it easy to buy from you in the way the consumer wants and expects it? Or are you withholding information or insisting they call you first? Understand this, nobody likes or wants to compete a "contact us" form....ever. Now there may be good reasons that you need to communicate with them to place an order. But understand that there is somebody out there trying to find a way of circumnavigating that and enabling people to buy online without any friction.

Take a look at your own buying process and look for these friction points where you make it difficult to buy and challenge it. Is it really a necessary step or can it be easier and simpler?

Defining and designing your sales process is a fundamental step in the new ways of selling. Map it out and understand what your prospects are trying to achieve at each stage of the process. Are they looking to answer a question? Do they have objections that stop them even considering your industry, product or service? Do they have fears or expectations that they need addressing?

Your digital footprint across all channels is a window into your company and each one plays a part in the story your prospect tells them about you. This is done subconsciously but do not doubt it happens. The same is true for your offline footprint. How often have you been cut up by a van or car driver that has commercial branding all over it? Rightly or wrongly this affects the way we feel about that brand as much as the driver. What about the overbearing sales person at the networking event who interrupted your conversation to shove his business card in your face? Again, this affects how you feel about the brand he is part of as much as the individual.

"In a world where we can buy from anyone, why should your prospects and customers choose you?" - Chris Brogan

Write that down and share it with your entire team. This is the new market we live in today - a global market place where innovation is looking to find a better way to do what you do, a faster and more efficient way that meets the needs of your customers.

CHAPTER 7 - DIGITAL

I called this chapter "Digital" as opposed to digital marketing because I see digital as so much more than just marketing. Digital is a primary channel that we default to as soon as we get a split second and stop thinking about the real world and the here and now. It's where we go when we start to wonder what's happened everywhere else and with everyone else.

Sure marketing is a huge component of digital but let's not only think about it as a marketing channel but more like another dimension that exists in our everyday lives. It is yet another place to be and another place to manage but like it or not, it's there and we are all part of it.

Take your music collection for example; now I never actually owned any records but I did own cassettes and remember CD's first coming to market. There was the initial uproar of having to buy your collections again on CD; then the same happened with MP3s and iTunes as we moved into the first stages of digital and owning your music in a digital way. However fast forward to today and we no longer want to store MP3s; we do not even want to own music we just want access. Music today is streamed to us on demand, when we want it and on whatever device is in front of us. The change that digital has created by being connected has disrupted and changed the music industry forever.

Digital comes with its own rules; although not actually governed by anyone, we all know how we should or should not behave in these channels and we give and take from it based on what we get from it overall.

I grew up in an era where not everybody had a colour TV. Changing the channel meant getting up and pressing a button and even tuning it in like a radio. Computers had green screens and it was safe to play outside your house with friends.

Today there are people that are in the workforce and even running businesses that have never known the world without the Internet and touch screen technology.

Millennials and Generation Z are from a connected era where communication is primarily digital and being connected is a given. They adopt technology quickly and are digitally competent.

Being digitally competent is not just for the younger generations but for all. Just because these people grew up with technology does not mean it is just for them. Digital is a way and a fabric of our everyday lives and applies to all. In order to stay relevant today being digitally competent is an essential skill set you need to embrace or face being left behind very quickly.

What does being digitally competent mean? It's really about understanding the basics; enough to be able to participate and communicate on whatever platform is relevant to you and your audience. It may be only one platform that makes the most sense to you right now, but be aware audiences and technology shift very quickly so be prepared to go wherever your audiences expect you to.

The tables have turned now and with

information available everywhere, and everyone being connected, no longer do brands push out messages and attract sales as easily as they used to.

We expect to get replies from brands on social networks and quickly too. At first brands were reluctant to join the party but soon realised that they were on there whether they liked it or not and so are you. Customer service is now a huge role and challenge for brands on social media. This is where people will talk about your products, services and people and they can say whatever they want.

Digital is the window into your company. It may have been a shop window before but now this window is whatever screen is in front of the consumer. This has changed how business is done for pretty much everyone. It has also changed our daily lives.

What is the last thing you touch before you go to bed at night? What is the first thing you touch in the morning? If it is your mobile phone do not worry too much as that is the case for most people, rightly or wrongly. This is an example of just how dependent we are on the digital channels and the utility they provide us. We are never more than a few feet away from our mobiles at best and now with smart watches being connected to them, the notifications and some data is being fed through to our wrist. How much longer will it before we are prepared to have technology surgically embedded into our bodies?

Digital is not always a direct like for like replacement for traditional media although many marketers would like to think that is the case. Spam email and Banner ads are the digital equivalents of junk mail and leaflets and they are just as unwelcome. Digital channels enable us to find what we want and yet still people are finding ways to push their messages onto us.

Some of the digital platforms and search engines are addressing this and are trying to create relevant experiences by using algorithms to filter what we see.

For business owners and marketers what

is important to understand is how savvy the modern consumer is. They often know more than the sales person as they have done their research. They are seeking feedback from friends and peers both personally and professionally. They know what the going rate is and more importantly they know where to look for good value. They also do not tolerate poor marketing. Getting somebody to subscribe to your email list is harder than ever. We are all over subscribed already and only let somebody into our inbox if they are prepared to offer value and utility. The moment somebody crosses the line or is no longer relevant we unsubscribe in a heartbeat.

To market in a digital first world brings amazing opportunity and challenges. So far we have covered attention spans and the new technology driven connected society. We understand how the tables have turned and the modern consumer has access to unthinkable amounts of information and the ability to access it anytime. This in turn has affected the way we buy and the way we sell.

Digital marketing has changed and is evolving every single day; what has not changed is that those who provide transparency, honesty, utility and a great product or service backed up with great support will thrive. Get those fundamentals right and worrying about marketing tactics is less of a problem. The reason is in today's digital and connected society your best sales people are your customers. There is very little that is more powerful than that of a happy customer telling others how wonderful you are. We trust our friends', family's and peers' opinions and reviews. Sure we will do our own due diligence but word of mouth and referrals have always being king way before digital, but they are far more visible and powerful today.

Digital marketing is still very young, despite email marketing being around for years. Social media has probably been the biggest and most disruptive and has changed personal relationships as much as business ones.

Trying to keep up with social and digital is almost impossible; my advice is to not try to keep up as it is a full time job. Understand what works for your business and master that before chasing the shiny bright object which is the new social media platform. There are many ways to measure social media and its effectiveness but I wouldn't get caught up in vanity metrics. You cannot pay the bills with Likes and Follows. Sure they are great but you should really be measuring depth of relationships you make and not amount of followers you accumulate.

There is an awful lot of noise on social media as the majority are using it as a mega phone to try to shout the loudest in the hope that they get heard. By concentrating on being helpful and useful, and by listening on social media, you can get huge value and insight. Treat each individual connection as you would a customer or a friend. Join each conversation with the intention of listening and adding value and measure the quality of the relationships and friends you make and not the likes and re-tweets.

Social media is just one important spoke in your digital marketing wheel. Your website, email, search engine optimization (SEO), blogging, video, podcasting and live streaming are all other spokes that make up your wheel. But which of these are important and which do you need to be concentrating on, if any?

The answer is quite simple; you need to do whatever your customers and prospects expect you to do. Let me explain a little more. Having the basics in place and getting those right is where most small businesses fail. They are too busy trying a bit of this and a bit of that and seeing which one can elevate their sales messages the loudest.

However what does your customer or prospect expect from you? They expect the basics and are often disappointed. So what are the basics? Let's start with your website.

Your website is not really yours. The biggest mistake people make is that they think the website is a place for them to brag and tell everyone how great they are. They also expect people to buy right now right there. Think about how you use a website when considering a product or service. In most B2B (Business to Business) and lots of B2C (Business to Consumer) examples, people research and will consume 10 - 15 resources before considering making a purchase. Does your website guide prospects to find the information they want, and fast? Does it answer their questions? Does it address their concerns and objections? Just like music, we are now digital buyers and we expect a self serve, on-demand experience. We want to be able to do our research and get the answers to our questions from your digital footprint and specifically on your website. I would suggest starting with your website and getting that right first. A well designed website takes users on a journey that they wanted to take, to find the information they want. A good user journey understand that not everybody is ready to buy today and serves up relevant content based on where they are in the sales process to help them rule themselves in or out; a website that enables people to buy when they are ready.

Have a content marketing strategy that nurtures prospects and educates them and empowers them to determine that you are the best fit for them and will support them. Content can be blog posts, videos, eBooks, podcasts and even website copy as well as everything offline. Position your company as a great teacher in your industry and answer every question you can possibly think of. This will create trust and demonstrate transparency, all the things we want in a supplier. Which types of content to produce is as simple as understanding which one answers the question the best? And which one you are most comfortable producing. If your audience do not listen to podcasts then do not produce one; although you will need to determine this before assuming. Podcasting is very much hot right now and an excellent way to communicate with your audience.

Producing lots of wonderful and helpful content is only one part of the process. As we know there is a vast amount of noise out there so how do you ensure your content is seen? You have to make your content work. Have a content distribution strategy that considers who your ideal audience is and where they expect to find the answers to their questions. It could be LinkedIn groups, or Facebook groups; it may be trade publications and even as simple as a Google search. The likelihood is it will be a number or all of those places. You need to find out where these places are and then ensure your content is seen there. This could involve building relationships with certain bloggers or editors in order to get access to their audiences. Over time, the strategy has to be having your own audience as well and you do that by ensuring you have systems in place to nurture these relationships. The system could be as simple as getting permission to email them by collecting their email address on your website. This is, again, not as easy as it used to be and often means you have to give something away in exchange for their email address. Using social media is another way to promote your content and bring people to your website. However, you will need to ensure that the content you are sharing is relevant and useful to your followers.

I could go on for days with different strategies for digital but this is not a book about digital; it is a book about evolving as a business. Understand that digital is the primary channel your customer and prospects use to communicate, collaborate, research, buy and sell. Mastering the digital channels is no longer something for the future but very much now.

CHAPTER 8 - DISRUPTION

We touched a tiny bit on disruption in Chapter 4 with how cloud computing is changing the face of many businesses.

However it is so much more than just cloud services; a combination of technology, the internet, and digital is powering innovation at a rapid rate.

Everywhere you look people are looking down at a screen of some kind. We are living huge parts of our lives in our smart phones. There is also a new scarcity on the block - time. Time is what we all seem to have less and less of. The reasons are many; ever since we started being paid by the hour we have associated time with money. We are all in a rush and with more inputs being thrown at us in the forms of text messages, voicemails, phone calls, emails, social media messages and notifications it is no wonder we are feeling stressed and time conscious. We no longer have those five minute gaps to day dream, every time we have 30 seconds to spare we reach for our smart phone.

FOMO (fear of missing out) plays a big part in this as does the reward or dopamine effect. The dopamine effect is the chemical that is released from the rewards centre of our brains; it also acts as a re-enforcer of a particular behaviour. Checking social media and email and then getting a little tit-bit of interesting information triggers this area of the brain and it makes us feel good even for just a nanosecond. This is the reason we keep scrolling endlessly on social streams in search of another tit-bit.

Every minute and second is accounted for. This is even more so in the western world where people are striving and working more and more hours despite the advancements in technology. We seem to be getting busier but is it that now we have more distractions and opportunities?

We are still at the very beginning of disruption and the next few years are going to be very bumpy as the world as we know it is already changing fast and shows no signs of slowing.

You have all seen the statements and stats

before but it gives a very clear sign of where we are heading.

Uber, the world's largest taxi company, owns no vehicles. Facebook, the world's most popular media owner, creates no content. Alibaba, the most valuable retailer, has no inventory and Airbnb, the world's largest accommodation provider, owns no real estate. Something interesting is happening.

These companies are all facilitators; they are using our connectedness to provide utility. These companies are all relatively young and most likely all told "it will never work".

It is not just these companies either that you need to think about; Instagram now owns the photo moment. Around 60 million photos are uploaded there every single day. Before that the company was Kodak which, at its peak, employed around 145,000 people worldwide. At the time of acquisition by Facebook, Instagram had just 13 employees and millions of users.

I appreciate that these are all large examples that most people are aware of. However these kinds of examples are happening every single day. Somewhere out there in the world is someone creating a new, faster more efficient, cost effective way of doing some part or all of what you offer.

Having skills is not enough anymore. There are people with amazing skills in all kinds of disciplines, operating in all kinds of places across the globe, who are prepared to provide them for less. Your website can be developed by anyone so can your app or design work or just about anything. With around 9 clicks I can order some amazing things to be manufactured with my logo on and shipped worldwide. All you need is a credit card. This is, of course, not true in every single discipline but even on a local level a few clicks or taps on my phone and all of your competitors' websites and phone numbers are in front of me.

We are becoming smarter with information and wherever there is a middle man there is inefficiency. That inefficiency is being removed and replaced every single day.

How long will it be until B&Q or someone new offer a service to mow your lawn and water your flowers for a fixed low cost monthly fee? With a few taps on the mobile have them fix the leaky tap and replace the broken fence panel? We can already have shopping delivered and Amazon now have a service called Dash where you can press a button on your washing machine and it then orders and delivers a pre-determined about of washing tablets and clothes conditioner from a single button press; the same with loo roll and all kinds of simple household items. Nest is now having us install smart devices in our homes so we can have the heating and hot water controlled from our phone. This is now being extended to your car so it knows how far away you are and can switch the oven on at the exact right time based on location and traffic. All of this due to the 'big data' we are creating every minute of every day.

It is not just inefficiency that is driving innovation but manual labour too.

Supermarkets with self serve checkouts are just one example of many more we can expect in the coming years. As discussed earlier, companies can do more with less people and where they can use technology to replace manual labour they will. We want everything quicker and easier and that is where we are heading. If your business is a middleman of any kind, then you need to look at where you are adding clear value to the process to justify it. Now we can connect direct to customers and on a global scale with ease, using third parties is less of a requirement than it was.

We are also giving more data to things like wearable technology via our smart phones which is measuring all kinds of things that in the coming years are going to become even scarier. We already have services where we can use a mobile app to talk to a private doctor. There is nothing stopping a virtual doctor sending you a message via your smart watch/phone or any other connected device to tell you in advance that there could be something wrong or you might be coming down with something based on the data you are sending them via your connected wearable devices.

Virtual sports coaches could be another possibility with data from your last work out or sports match. The possibilities are endless.

Whatever industry you are in today you need to consider what is disrupting you today, tomorrow and even better *be the disruptor*. Lead the conversation around change and what it means for your customers and your industry. Yes things have been pretty simple for the last 50 years but as of now, everything is up for change.

I get it, you have built your career to date based on the old rules and now you are being asked to change. This is not just for the kids anymore as those millennials are now in the work place and even starting companies.

I am not writing this to tell you it's fair or wrong or right, just that it is. This is not a fad and things are never going back to the good old days. Innovation is just starting and what was new last year could be gone tomorrow. Embracing change and keeping up is now the status quo.

CHAPTER 9 - LEADERSHIP

How is leadership different in this new digital and connected era? It starts with acceptance that this is all very real and we are not returning to the good old days. I say this because there are still lots of business owners I meet after many of my talks who say they enjoyed my talk but they are not ready to re-learn how to run a business and how to do sales and marketing in a mobile first and digital world.

I get it; they have worked very hard to build a business and now it is all change. However this change is not a one off now. Change is something we have to get used to every day, month and year from now. I could argue that in fact the business principals of today of honesty, integrity, fairness and transparency are in fact not new at all and have been the foundations of many successful businesses. The only difference is the delivery of that and the understanding of how consumers and prospects now buy.

In order to be a successful leader today you need be on-top of all of these business challenges and disruptions. Understanding how technology is impacting your industry and maybe even your business direct is of up-most importance. You do not need to know how the technology works so much as its impact. By understanding how other industries are being disrupted, and in some cases wiped out completely, you will be in a much better position to foresee these changes and maybe even lead the changes.

This is not about learning social media and ticking a box; it is understanding what is social and every other technology and how it affects your business, staff, suppliers, competitors and everything in-between. It is about being an engaged leader; looking at using this technology to your advantage and not using age as a barrier or excuse. This is not about the kids and generation Y and Z but as Brian Solis calls it, "Generation C" for connected. Generation C can be any age and in any position in life and business. This generation use technology in their daily life to improve and enhance their experience. More importantly as a leader in the digital era you should understand the importance of the word 'experience'. We live in a world where everybody has permission to publish and tell the world what they think. Through social media and personal blogs, getting your opinion into the public arena has never been easier. What this means is that your prospects' and customers' experience starts way before your team gets to speak to them and continues through any sales process, becoming a customer, throughout the time they remain a customer and in some cases for long after.

Every interaction with your brand forms part of that experience. Some of these are online and others are offline but they all make up the overall experience. As a leader, it is your job to understand this and put in place the plans and strategies to create and manage these experiences. However, if you are not an engaged leader who embraces the new ways of doing business, how can you lead those who are creating and engaging with your prospects and customers?

There is no place for a bad business to exist any longer. Review sites and social media have made it really easy for prospects to see what people really think about your company, staff and products. There are, of course issues with review sites, but that does not mean they can be ignored.

One of the biggest challenges digital has created and leaders need to understand is how different we communicate today than even just 5 years ago. There are so many different channels and we have very little control of any of them. As a leader, you will need to know where your customers are communicating and where your staff are as well. Some of the more digitally savvy leaders have implemented communication plans and internal platforms to manage this. By both communicating and listening on internal systems like Yammer and Podio, you can communicate in real time and get useful feedback and information. I believe that these systems will be very important in teams of all sizes and, in particular, as we embrace the remote worker more and more.

How does this scale you might ask yourself? In the case of larger teams or even time pressed leaders, it is not so much about listening and reading everything from everybody, but about listening and following those that do read and listen to everything. This gives you the information you need in the shortest amount of time. This is all about listening at scale.

The next step is to share via digital channels in order to lead. By creating valuable information (which doesn't always have to be written by you) that highlights and reinforces your message you can lead through the digital channels. This could be staff or it could be people you influence via social media.

You will then have to engage where appropriate and if not you, then via others in the business when and where it makes sense. There are times where you can spot amazing opportunities to jump in and engage where a customer may not be expecting it and it can make a huge difference. For example, if somebody is complaining via a social media channel about your company, people, product or services they may not expect the owner to join the conversation. But by doing so and letting them know that you are hearing them and will see that this issue is sorted can have a profound effect. As customers we just want to know we are being heard.

Of course this example cannot be done each and every single time but for certain situations it can be a fantastic tool.

There is a wealth of knowledge and information available to us all today and by being a connected and engaged leader you can communicate and lead at scale far easier than ever before. Yes it involves a new mindset and possibly new skills but by understanding the way we all communicate today and how we can leverage technology to help us build better relationships and better businesses, you will be more than ready to lead in this digital era.

CHAPTER 10 - EDUCATION

You may think this is an odd chapter in a business book. Education was something you did when you were younger and that's it right? Not in today's information age. With the rapid rate of change comes a massive amount of new information and ways of doing things. In order to keep up requires an ongoing education.

The traditional education system was designed to manage and educate the masses. It also taught us to look for the right answer and to do things one way. This resulted in producing the required type of worker we needed at that time - the factory worker. The traditional education system was designed and rolled out around the time of the industrial revolution and so naturally was designed to create the kind of workers that society needed most. Management styles were also developed around the need to manage factory workers and were built around efficiency, cost effectiveness and getting more from less. This required more compliance and less creativity.

Today requires a very different type of worker and mindset. Today many of the brightest and smartest employees and entrepreneurs are pushing back on how we used to do things. They see new ways of doing things and often challenge the status quo. They understand that we are in a new era and a society full of opportunity. Everything that was, is no longer. Everything is up for grabs and the way we do pretty much everything can be, and is being, challenged. There is no right answer and we seek to fail fast in order to learn and keep things lean. We need to start re-wiring our brains to think more creatively and be willing to push more boundaries if we want to evolve. Some of the greatest minds and innovations of our time were because of such refusal to accept no as an answer, to keep trying and failing and learning. The motor industry would not be where it is today if Henry Ford had taken the first few responses of "it cannot be done". Despite a year of being told this he pushed back and said keep trying until they found a way. We have been stifled into thinking about the one and only right answer in order to pass a test or get a tick or get picked, yet today the rewards come to those who push back and ask themselves, "can this be done better?" Now as a business owner you can choose to ignore this and stick to traditional methods but just be aware the world has changed and your staff have changed. The new wave of employees and business owners expect different ways of working and thinking.

The old promise of study hard, get good grades, go to college and university then get a job for life is now more farfetched than ever before. People are not only changing jobs many times over their career but they are changing careers altogether as they learn new things and change passions. We were asked to make decisions about our vocation at 16 years old that often would take us down a path for the next 20 years before many wake up and realize that this is not what they want to do any longer. This is why many people make sudden career changes and often deviate completely from their original degree subject. Even the idea of full time employment is coming into question. With so much regulation and red tape it is not easy to employ and manage lots of people. There is a change we are going through right now with the rise of the freelancer. In 1995, 93% of the workforce were either full or part time employees. This remained throughout and into the early 2000s until five years ago when we began to see a shift. Today, around 15% of the market are freelancers and this figure is expected to continue to rise to around 20% of the market by 2020. The ability to connect and work from home with people all over the world has enabled a new kind of work for individuals. Many of these freelancers work for many different companies and have a better quality of life too. This works for many companies as they do not have the hassle of HR and everything that comes with employment. This model is not new and is becoming more popular. The film industry has worked this way for years where teams are formed for a project and then separate after. Some come back together for other projects and sometimes with different people. This will not suit all people or employers but it is happening and the freelance economy is both an opportunity and a threat.

Today, education is not something you do once but something we need to doing throughout our career. I am not suggesting formal education but a natural curiosity and eagerness to learn more and keep current. As business leaders this is more important than ever. It is not always about understanding everything in great detail, but understanding enough to see how it could impact your business or improve it. Finding time to dedicate to ongoing education is imperative. Listen to audio books or podcasts in the car or schedule time to keep up to date with the latest trends and blogs in your industry. Invest in online courses, read books or whatever format works for you. And when you find something that resonates, share it with your leadership teams and staff members. You will need to encourage your staff to remain curious and allow them time to learn. Not everyone will want to, but those that do will take your business forward. There is, of course, the risk they will get better and want to leave. If this is the case, you can either try to accommodate their needs where it makes sense for the business or you must let them fly and encourage them to soar. There is no point trying to keep people in roles they are not suited for; the right bums on the right seats.

Being digitally proficient is not about being under 30 and good on social media. It is about being savvy and educated enough to be able to understand digitals impact on your business both today and tomorrow. This is not just for business leaders but for all your team. Make sure you understand why and how you use any social and digital technologies in your organisation

CHAPTER 11 - PRIVACY

Privacy is a really hot and debated topic these days and for good reason. The Internet has brought with it some fantastic and life changing benefits. It has also brought with it huge amounts of disruption and challenges. As technology companies are finding more and more ways to get attention and knowledge about their potential prospects, they are also collecting huge amounts of data about you and me. Have you ever noticed that advert following you around the Internet for days, and sometimes weeks, on end? You may have asked yourself how they know the items you have been looking at and/or how they follow you around. If you have not noticed it before, simply go to Amazon and take a look at something and then without buying it, take notice when you visit Facebook or other sites that exact product is sitting there in the advert suggesting you buy it. This is called re-targeting or re-marketing. It works by placing a little file on your computer when you visit their site called a cookie. Then, when you visit other sites, the information stored in the cookie tells the re-targeting provider who you are and what product you were looking at. If that site has adverts used by that re-targeting provider it will then serve up the advert of the product you were looking at.

Creepy, huh? This is just the tip of the iceberg as to what websites know about us and what we do on their sites. Now, in some cases, the information collected is anonymous and in other cases it is not anonymous but used to make your browsing experience better. There is a fine line though between what is genuinely helpful and what is downright stalking.

The positive side of this is when the information collected makes our experience personalised; for example when a form is filled out for us or information we need to type in often is remembered. The Internet without personalisation is actually not a very good experience at all. The issue lies in what companies do with the data that they collect. Is it used to understand your user journeys with the aim of improving your experience or is it used to then send more adverts to you until you agree to buy?

If re-targeting spooked you a little, then this next section may or may not scare the life out of you, depending on what you expect or know about Facebook. When you join Facebook and tick the box that agrees to their terms and conditions, they make it very clear that they will be collecting data on you and using that data for various reasons including making your experience a better one. They are not hiding this information; I just don't believe people are actually reading those terms and conditions, nor anyone's for that matter. Now think, for a minute, about all the information you give to Facebook: your date of birth, location, friends, family, sports teams, music, film and books you like, where you go on holiday, where you go to dinner and god knows what else. People have their whole life on Facebook and a witness to their life. Now imagine how targeted an advert can be when Facebook knows all of this information about you. Now Facebook do state that they do not sell your data and never will; you can also control what happens with your data quite simply. Facebook are not doing anything illegal or wrong at all, but you may have thought that Facebook was free when in reality, by using their system, they are using your information to enable their advertisers to try and sell stuff to you based on your exact profile that you willingly gave them. This is pretty much true of any social network and not just Facebook.

There are many examples of information being collected, sold and shared. For example your credit card data may well be available for companies to buy. Again, depending on the terms and conditions with your credit card, it may well be the case that a certain amount of information like your purchases and amounts may be available to other third parties. This could be anonymous and trends be built around it or it could be that people can find out what you spend your money on and where.

Other examples of data tracking are with marketing automation solutions. Not only can a website track and store your journey through a website but it can, in some cases, track the emails you open and links you click as well. The same cookie tracking is used as well as the information your computer, smart phone or tablet tells the marketing system about you. For example your PC often uses what is known as an IP address to identify you on the Internet; some systems have the ability to see where your IP address is coming from and give the system a pretty good idea of where you are located in the world. Other more advanced systems will go a step further and if they can combine all of the above with your email address they can then track you in lots of places. They do this by getting you to identify yourself by giving the website your email address. Then across the different technologies they can see what pages you look at on their site, how you found the site and when and what emails they send you that you open. I think most people are aware that this happens and as long as there is a fair transaction normally in the form of an eBook or whitepaper or access to other parts of the site most people are aware and accept this trade of data.

I believe that as long as you are transparent and make people aware of what you are doing with their information and/or provide a high level of utility in exchange, such as Facebook or any other social network then most people are generally accepting of these practices. As a business owner, if you intend to use some of these systems and technologies just be aware of people's tolerance to how they feel they are being treated and how their data is being used. Often it is when a person is not expecting a level of personalisation that they feel "creeped out". Be aware of what data you have been given by a person and what data you have collected or researched. Telling someone that you know the colour of their front door because they gave you their postcode is going to cross the line. Personalisation can be a good thing and build rapport, but when done wrongly or taken too far it simply makes people uncomfortable.

When we are asked for information in exchange for your content such as an e-book or a Whitepaper or even access to gated video content, we are often offered two different options. The first being a traditional form to complete. These forms often ask for lots of information in exchange for the content on offer. Consumers today have to make the decision about the value of the content in exchange for their personal details. This means that the content is not free at all as there is a value attached to our personal information and we all know that we are going to be treated as a sales lead regardless of our reason or intent in downloading the content. There are some cases where I am just not willing to give certain information in exchange for content; often it is my phone number. In fact the more fields that are asked to be completed the less likely the form will be finished. The second option is a social sign in one. This is where you are offered the chance to download the content or create an account using an existing social media account. This of course is often convenient and means you do not need to complete any forms and in a few clicks you have access to the content. What you are actually doing is giving the content provider access to your basic information on that social network. For example if you choose to use Facebook as a social sign in, you may be then allowing your full name, date of birth and email address to be given to the content provider.

They may also get the amount of social connections you have too. Now what information gets exchanged is changing all of the time and varies by social network. But again social sign in is not free and never was. Understand that in today's digital environment, data is a currency.

CHAPTER 12 - PEOPLE AND SKILLS

Today offers a very different challenge with regard to the skills we require in order to thrive and not just survive. The path was always very clear previously as you got your required education; you then paid your dues and worked your way up in a company picking up the required skills as you went. Not so much today; there are many examples of entrepreneurs creating products and services and completely avoiding the traditional route. Some of these people are under 30 years old and find themselves managing teams of people that are potentially older and more experienced than them.

Likewise many leaders today are finding themselves with staff members that are under 24 years old and have very different views and expectations about the workplace and how things are done in general. Age is no longer a barrier to being a business owner or a skilled C-Level executive. This works both ways though and those leaders that embrace change and the new ways of doing business will find that experience really can make all the difference. They still need to understand the new world and even more so embrace it and master it. In order to do that, leaders will need to learn a whole bunch of new skills but in particular to understand and manage change.

Change is going to be the new constant going forward. Now I know lots of people struggle with change and just want things to go back to the good old days, trust me on this one, we are never going back, rightly or wrongly. There are many reasons why smart phones have formed many bad habits and ruined the way we act in public and the way we communicate. It has also opened the door to many new relationships and today people rely on their mobiles phones. I would go as far to say as people are without a doubt addicted to their mobile phones. Could you imagine trying to take away people's smart phones now? For better or worse it is here and it is never going back! The best thing we can do is adapt and learn to live with the constant of change and innovation that shows no signs of slowing down.

Other skills that people will benefit from going forward include keeping abreast of social trends and technologies. Do not try to keep up, just be aware of them. Keeping up with social media and other digital trends is a full time job. But by understanding where your audience is, or potentially is, could be is vital.

Having a personal brand or not is a heavily debated topic. Many small business owners may not like the idea of their employees having a personal brand in fear that they are raising their own profile instead of their employer's brand. This is understandable, although possibly a little short-sighted. If your employees have an audience and want to demonstrate their key skills being implemented they are likely to share brand stories and case studies. More often than not, employees will link back their current employer across social channels and in particular platforms like LinkedIn.

For many years brands fought against social media creeping into the workplace and it was a futile battle. You can block social media sites being accessed from your employees' desktop computers but you cannot stop them accessing it via their own smart phones which are often armed with 4G connections. Social media is a set of skills that is essential to the modern worker. Being present on the channels where you find your friends, family and the topics of conversation about the subjects you like, is now set as part of our culture. Sure employees may access it during work time but you will often find that they will also share your company updates and get involved in the conversations around it too. Embrace it and, where it makes sense, leverage your employees' social capital.

As for social media in your company, this is of course something you should do. It is something you are part of if you like it or not and your customers will expect and even demand you to be part it. I would be very surprised if me telling you that social media is an important function and skill set that is required is new. One thing I will mention is that social media is not something that is run by an under 21 or the youngest person in your company.   It is also not just a marketing function; it affects the leadership team, the customer service team, the sales team and the marketing team. Now it might be that you do all of those things? If you do, add social media manager to your list. Having a social media policy is important and this needs to be driven by the leadership team and shared and understood by your employees. Set some guidelines as to what is acceptable and what is not, as well as the vision for how social media is going to be leveraged by the organization to help drive awareness, education and sales for the brand.

Keeping in theme with this book, not embracing social media is a dangerous game. This is where people's attention is and this is where they spend every single second of their down time including walking between meetings and sitting on the loo.

I also believe that skills are easily learned but passion and attitude are not. Sometimes somebody can be skilled in their job but if they are not a good fit for the company culture it simply does not work. Finding people who are passionate about their role and have the right kind of attitude will be key to your growth in certain positions. Train for skills and hire for attitude.

Being more technically minded is becoming more of a necessity. For example, previously a small business marketing person would not have been expected to be overly technical but more creative and organized. They would not have built the company website but would have been involved from a creative perspective. Today, although not always required, many small business marketers do have a basic working knowledge of Wordpress and need to understand SEO and other marketing related technologies.

Technology is creeping into every area of business and having some of the basic skills can take you a long way today. The same can be said for small business owners. Understanding how pivotal technology is in the day to day running of your business is essential. When the Internet connection dies at the office, productivity slows to a halt. It's even worse if it happens in your home and you have teenage children.

In schools today, coding is becoming a serious topic and is considered a major language like any other. They have recognized how important a skill this is for the future of work and credit to them for integrating it into the curriculum.

Time is a most valued commodity today and in order to keep up you will need to make time for study in the form of courses and books. Even a few pages a day will lead you to 12 books a year and provide you with more knowledge than your competitors. Also for employees, this is a time when technology is taking over more and more jobs each and every year. Ask yourself, is your role potentially replaceable by technology? Which queues do you use at the supermarket? The self serve options or the traditional ones served by people? Rightly or wrongly, technology will replace many jobs and many industries so keeping yourself ahead of this is vital.

There are many stories and suggestions

that there will come a point where there is a serious job shortage due to technology and although there maybe some truth in this eventually, I also see opportunity for new jobs, new roles and new skills as a result of this change.

CHAPTER 13 - WHAT IS NEXT?

What is next? Who knows is the honest answer, but one thing for sure is that it is just around the corner and change will be the new constant. This is a really unique moment in time in that many of the rules are being broken or becoming irrelevant. I believe that in the next few years we will see huge strides and innovation in the smart/connected home. With more and more of our home and possessions becoming connected to the Internet it brings with it huge change and opportunity.

The changes will be more utility-based at first, like being able to see the water level of your kettle and then boil it, all from your smart phone. Smart ovens already exist today that cook your food perfectly and automatically. I can see huge increases in the use of voice activated devices like Siri that mean we start talking to our smart devices more and use them as a personal assistant. Again this technology is here already but I can see it becoming more intelligent and more universal.

The rise of wearable technology has already seen huge amounts of data being produced. This data is allowing the medical profession to gain a much deeper and more accurate understanding of our state of health. I can see in the very near future a time where your doctor will contact you requesting an appointment because of the data we have provided them via our wearable technology. Intelligent algorithms would have been able to spot trends and vital triggers that notify both you and your doctor.

Another area I can see making huge strides that will change the way we live is in the automobile industry. Both with the self driving car and the connected car already in production the way we travel is going to change significantly in the next 5 -10 years. Telematics are already becoming more and more popular and soon they will be mandatory but for how long they remain relevant is anyone's guess. I imagine the self driving car will make this redundant at some point but not before our insurance companies are billing us by the day as they have the data to show how well or not we are driving.

With regards to business change I can see some turbulent times ahead for those that do not make the necessary changes required to keep up with today's consumers and technology changes. As attention shifts to various different places so will the technology with it. Today our smart phone is becoming the remote control to our lives; how this device adapts and involves will very much dictate where we go next.

There is little or no point in trying to be 100% up-to date with social media as firstly it's a full time job and secondly your customers and prospects will not be there right away. Right now in 2016 messaging apps is where the attention is and is taking more and more time and attention away from social media. How do you market in messaging apps? This is a question that brands and agencies are working out now.

Many things will remain a constant throughout all of this technology innovation. Building relationships, trust and great teaching will remain at the core of most of these changes. How we access content and what content even looks like is a really interesting debate. But keeping these key components at the heart of your marketing and sales process will be key.

I can foresee a rise in the freelance market in the coming years as more people strive to achieve a greater work, life balance.

The Internet has given birth to many on-line market places that connect freelancers and companies together for varying amounts of money and quality. The fact is that we can all collaborate and communicate far easier than ever before and with people all over the world.

Video is without a doubt becoming a huge part of our daily content consumption with more and more video content being consumed than any other media type. It is not about just producing one video and sticking it on your website, but an ongoing process of creating content that inspires, informs and educates. This must all be part of telling not just your brand story, but understanding the role you play in your customer's story.

Access and not ownership is already a big player in 2016 as we do not want to own as much stuff as we did. We do however want access when we want it. We went from owning music and video content to downloading it but still having a copy to now just streaming it to wherever we are and on whatever device we happen to have.

One thing that all small business owners need to understand is that this is all just the very start. There are already examples where fairly new start-ups that disrupted an entire industry are being challenged themselves with new business models using new technologies. This is all built around convenience and lower barriers to entry. Being able to move fast when all the information and more importantly customers vote with their wallets is key, but again always with one eye on the future and what could be a better, faster, more cost effective way to serve your clients.

Be prepared to continuously be talking

with your customers and listening to what they are looking to achieve. Be prepared to always be testing and learning more about what works and what does not. Be prepared to be open-minded about new partnerships and new ways of serving your audience and your clients to meet their needs today. Understand that your prospects and customers have a voice and expect to be heard.

It is not all change everywhere though. If you are decent people providing a relevant service or product who looks after their clients and spends time educating their prospects then customers will always find you. Word of mouth is still very much alive and technology only makes it spread quicker and wider.

Yes the world has changed and will continue to change, but it also brings so much opportunity. There has never been a better time to start a business in history. The tools and resources available today for very little cost are amazing. The rules have changed and we are now all publishers and require no permission. If you stand out and are patient and put the work in then the new business landscape is an exciting place to be in. Many small business owners will continue to run their business exactly the same way as they have for years. Maybe they will dabble in social media and consider themselves digital but I can assure you there is so much more to it than that. This is where the opportunity is. There are huge gaps in many industries where they are not creating amazing experiences for their customers and are leaving the door open for someone else to come in and finish the job. Create value, create experiences that customers love and will want to talk about. Find new ways to serve them and in ways that make working with you as simple and as easy as possible. Remember people will pay for convenience, we want access not ownership, we want all inclusive, we don't want limits.

If you can leverage technology to find new ways to serve your audience, offer something different and place them as the hero in their story, then the future should not be scary at all. The future is here today and these are the new rules of doing business and those that evolve, like generations of humans before us, will thrive in the new landscape and those that don't will simply become obsolete.

ACKNOWLEDGMENTS

This book would not have been possible without many people. Some in my life in their carbon form and others in a virtual capacity, but each and every one as important as the next.

From my family at home who have had to put up with my late nights working on this and to my friends who encouraged me to write this book and pushed me to finish it.

Thank you also to my launch team who are helping me spread the word and see if we can help as many small business owners as possible take the required steps to ensure that their business is ready to adapt and evolve and continue to provide value and remain profitable.

To all the experts and authors who have no idea how they have impacted me with their own work and books and helped me learn more everyday and remain a student forever.

In particular I would like to acknowledge the following people who without would not have made this book possible:

Michelle King - My editor - Michelle has made this book readable and something I am proud to publish - Thank you - If you want an amazing editor you can contact Michelle at mlking@live.co.uk

Derek Doepker -from www.ebookbestsellersecrets.com - Self publishings best kept secret - This guy is a real rock star :-)

Nathan Dasco - from http://ecoverdesignerpro.com/coverdesign/

Sally Marshall for believing in me every step of the way

Dave McRobbie - A real friend and supporter

And course my family :-)

If this book has impacted you in a positive

way in any shape or form then please let me know - david@davidmarkshaw.com

Join my mailing list to hear more about this subject matter in my blogs, podcasts and future books.

And if you feel so compelled to do so I would be very grateful for a review on Amazon to help me make a positive impact for more people.

Dont forget you can get free access to the companian course that comes with this book by signing up at www.davidmarkshaw.com/book-course